EDGE BOOKS

Unusual
and
Awesome
JOBS
in
MATH

Stunt Coordinator,
Cryptologist,
and More

by Lisa M. Bolt Simons

CAPSTONE PRESS
a capstone imprint

Edge Books are published by Capstone Press,
1710 Roe Crest Drive, North Mankato, Minnesota 56003
www.capstonepub.com

Library of Congress Cataloging-in-Publication Data
Simons, Lisa M. B., 1969–
  Unusual and awesome jobs using math : stunt coordinator, cryptologist, and more / by Lisa
M. Bolt Simons.
      pages cm. — (You get paid for THAT?)
  Includes bibliographical references.
  ISBN 978-1-4914-2030-0 (Hardcover)
  ISBN 978-1-4914-2201-4 (eBook PDF)
1. Mathematics — ocational guidance —Juvenile literature. 2. Mathematicians — Juvenile
literature. 3. Occupations — Juvenile literature. I. Title.
  QA10.5.S56 2015
  510.23 — dc23   2014040360ISBN 978-1-4914-2030-0

Editorial Credits
Editor: Nate LeBoutillier
Designer: Veronica Scott
Media researcher: Jo Miller
Production specialist: Tori Abraham

Photo Credits
Alamy: AF Archive, 10-11, age fotostock Spain, S.L./Javier Larrea, 13, All Canada Photo/
Rich Wheater, 17, Paul Fleet, 7; Getty Images: AFP/Leon Neal, 19, 29; NASA, 4-5, James
Blair, 15; Newscom: EPA/Uli Deck, 22, Getty Images/AFP/John MacDougall, 20-21, Reuters/
Jason Reed, 27; Photoshot: Cultura/Image Source, 25; Science Source: Philippe Psaila, 9;
Shutterstock: Inga Nielsen, cover (background), iurii, cover (astronaut), lynea, cover (brain),
Maksim Kabakou, cover (background)

Printed in the United States of America in North Mankato, Minnesota.
052015   008968R

TABLE OF CONTENTS

BEYOND NUMBERS

Do you think math is fun? Many challenging, unusual, and yes, even fun jobs using math are out there for hire.

Cryptologists need math to unlock secrets. Astronauts and avalanche researchers need math way up high. Some math jobs, such as stunt coordinator or animator, may involve the world of entertainment. Other jobs, such as robotics engineer or visual effects supervisor, use math to bring things of the imagination to reality. The following jobs may someday be your mathematical career of choice.

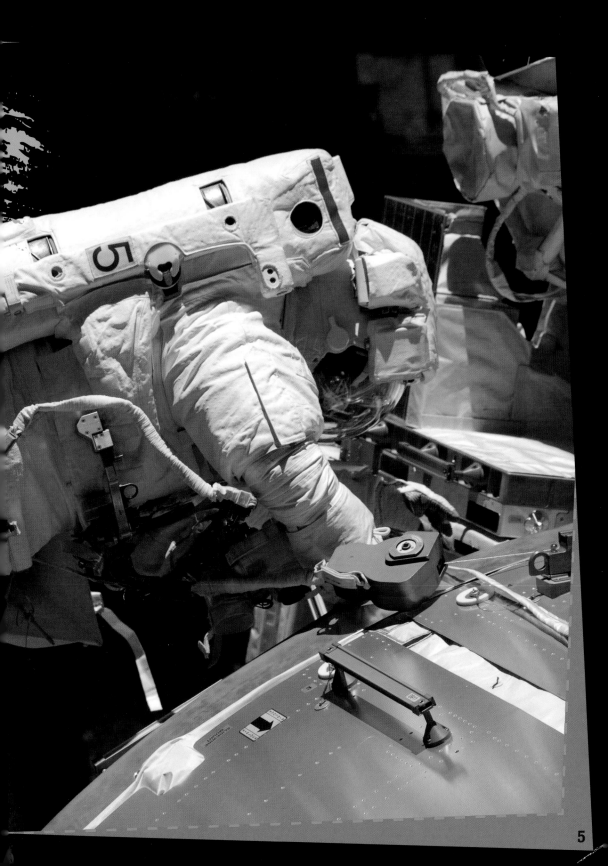

CRIMINALIST

Special Skills: extremely sanitary, curious, communicative

Education: bachelor's degree; advanced degrees may be necessary

Prior Experience: none

Hourly Schedule: varies; may be regular full-time hours or graveyard shift (night hours)

Salary: $53,000 per year on average

Many TV shows feature criminalists, or **forensic** specialists. Solving crimes in an hour is not realistic. Tests, data analyses, and reports include time-consuming trigonometry, geometry, algebra, and **statistics**.

Criminalists have three main jobs. One is to determine probabilities. For example, in one blood sample, what is the chance the DNA pattern repeats in other people, 1 in 100 or 1 in 1 million? Another job is to calculate the quantity to sample, such as in illegal drug cases.

The last job is to study a crime scene. For instance, when blood spatters, a stain is formed. The stain's shape depends on the angle of impact. The length and width of the stain helps calculate that angle. The angle of impact and the blood spatter patterns help the criminalist determine what happened.

forensic—relating to the use of scientific knowledge or methods in solving crimes

statistics—information, or data, that is collected and analyzed

EVIDENC

YOU'D BETTER BELIEVE IT!

Female blowflies find bodies minutes after death. They lay about 250 eggs where it's damp and warm, like in a victim's nose. In 1936 Dr. Alexander Mearns brought maggots to a murder trial to help establish the time of victims' deaths.

Branches of Mathematics

trigonometry	the study of the properties of triangles and straight sides
geometry	deals with points, lines, angles, surfaces, and solids
algebra	uses letters to represent numbers in equations
probability	concerning the likelihood of possible outcomes

ANIMATOR

Special Skills: artistic, precise, and deadline-oriented

Education: bachelor's degree; master's degree may be helpful

Prior Experience: none unless you want to work on full-length movies, then you need prior studio experience

Hourly Schedule: usually regular full-time hours; nights or weekends when a project is nearing completion

Salary: $61,000 per year starting

Drawing in class during an algebra lesson may get you into trouble. However, both math and artistic ability can lead to a career as an animator.

Winsor McCay, Emile Cohl, Georges Melies, and Walt Disney worked on moving pictures in the early 1900s. They needed algebra to make characters larger or smaller. They used trigonometry to make the characters seem alive.

Some animators still draw the **storyboard** with pencil, paper, and maybe a ruler. But most of today's cartoons and movies are created on computers.

First, animators build models. They use geometric shapes like triangles, cubes, cylinders, and spheres. Then they bend and twist the shapes. The models are then moved into three-dimensional (3-D) space using coordinates like x, y, and z. Animation computer programs look like electronic graphs with numbers, negative signs, and decimals.

storyboard—a series of drawings that shows the plot of a TV show or movie

An animator working with LEGO ® bricks for an action scene.

Other animators create the layout, or the placement, on the computer. Surfaces and shapes appear smooth by using geometry. Making the characters move involves solving equations. Adding lighting and shading uses **calculus**.

Most animators who want to work on full-length movies need to start as junior animators. With experience, animators can become lipsync artists, lead animators, animation supervisors, animation directors, and series directors.

Cartoons and movies aren't the only jobs for animators. Fields such as medicine, home construction, aerospace, advertising, and forensics may also use professional animators. Animators may need to create animated training sessions or client presentations.

calculus—a branch of mathematics that helps determine how things change

FLUID MECHANICS RESEARCHER

HELP WANTED

Special Skills: self-discipline and the ability to analyze, interpret, and reason

Education: master's degree; doctorate degree important for research

Prior Experience: none but projects in college can be helpful

Hourly Schedule: regular full-time hours

Salary: $20,000 to more than $100,000

How many nutrients does your body absorb after eating a candy bar versus a banana? (Your mom might want to know.) How much blood pumps through a giraffe's jugular vein? (A zookeeper might want to know.) To find the answers, fluid mechanics researchers and engineers use **estimation**, **ratios**, and statistics.

Professionals in this field also use special equations just for fluid. These equations are difficult to solve because of **turbulence** in the flow of fluid. Time, space, and speed, which are always changing, also affect the results.

Besides food digestion and blood flow, fluid mechanics researchers and engineers may also focus on fluids in ocean currents or land irrigation. They may also study gases in space and flight.

estimation—a guess made by using the information you have
ratio—a comparison of two quantities or numbers using division
turbulence—flow or motion that is not regular or normal

ASTRONAUT

Special Skills: excellent physical condition; willingness to travel and be gone from home for long periods of time; if going to the International Space Station, ability to speak Russian

Education: bachelor's degree in math, engineering, or science; master's degree preferred; up to two years of astronaut training

Prior Experience: three years in the field; military background, K-12 teaching experience, research experience, engineering, or medical background; pilots must have 1,000 hours in a jet aircraft

Hourly Schedule: when on a mission, anytime you're not sleeping

Salary: $50,790 to $130,810 for civilian astronauts; salaries of military astronauts are not disclosed

For the United States the space shuttle era ended the summer of 2011. But space travel is not over. Astronauts still need to travel to and from the International Space Station (ISS). This laboratory has orbited Earth since 2000. Future space travel includes plans to land on Mars and an asteroid.

Math is used for almost all of astronauts' duties. Some astronauts estimate fuel loads and weights. Others measure samples for ISS experiments. Monitoring the life support systems on the ISS involves ratios, percentages, and **deviations**. Astronauts may also calculate speed and distance for flights.

If you can be in tight spaces, avoid motion sickness, and are not afraid of heights, this may be the job for you. But there is stiff competition for the job. After training you need to be one of the eight candidates chosen out of about 6,000 applicants.

deviation—in statistics the difference between one quantity and the expected or normal quantity

AVALANCHE RESEARCHER

Do you like the outdoors in winter? How about statistics? If you enjoy both, an avalanche researcher could be your dream job.

Avalanche researchers can work at a university, laboratory, or mountain destination known for avalanches. They study current weather and weather history to estimate the chances of an avalanche. These probabilities also use the geometric concept of **slope**. The slope of the mountain is analyzed with wind and the snow's water content. Avalanche research professionals also look at data to figure out trends. All of this information can be used to prevent avalanches.

Though their computers do a lot of the calculating, researchers must understand the math. If they don't, it's hard to catch errors or bad results. Training others in safety precautions is another part of the job.

slope—in geometry, the steepness of a line

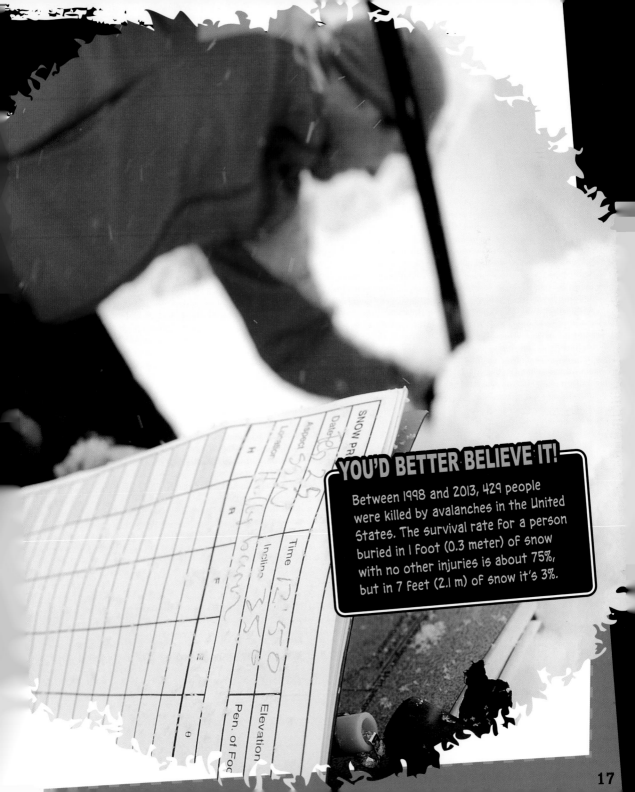

SNOW PR...

Date:

Aspect

Location

H

R

F

E

θ

Time

Incline

Elevation

Pen. of Foo...

12:50

356

ROBOTICS ENGINEER

Special Skills: detailed, imaginative, and team-oriented

Education: bachelor's degree; master's degree or doctorate preferred

Prior Experience: other engineering fields; robotics experience

Hourly Schedule: regular full-time hours; some overtime when working on a project or approaching a deadline

Salary range: $50,000 to $120,000

Long before robots were invented, a Greek mathematician named Archytas built an **automaton** in the late 300s BC. It was in the shape of a dove. Historians believe that Archytas' dove "flew" from one roost to another on a pulley. Archytas needed to know geometry in order to build this mechanical bird.

Besides geometry, today's robotics engineers also need algebra and calculus. Algebra includes different equations and **matrices**. Calculus includes **integrals** to figure out area and volume. Engineers need all this math to design, test, maintain, and improve robots. Computers do a lot of the math calculations. But a robotics engineer needs to know if the answers are correct.

At first robots were used in manufacturing companies with assembly lines. Now robots can carry out more jobs that might be boring or even dangerous. Some robots disarm bombs or handle unsafe material. Others just vacuum.

automaton—a mechanical or moving object built centuries ago

matrix—in linear algebra, numbers in an array, or numbers in rows and columns

integral—one of the two most basic concepts in calculus that helps determine area, volume, and lengths

A modern rover named "Bridget" could be used to navigate the surface of the planet Mars.

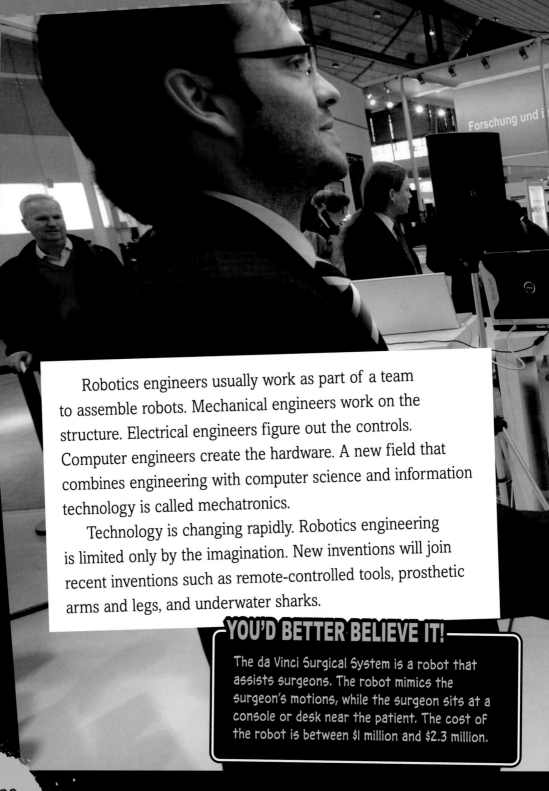

Robotics engineers usually work as part of a team to assemble robots. Mechanical engineers work on the structure. Electrical engineers figure out the controls. Computer engineers create the hardware. A new field that combines engineering with computer science and information technology is called mechatronics.

Technology is changing rapidly. Robotics engineering is limited only by the imagination. New inventions will join recent inventions such as remote-controlled tools, prosthetic arms and legs, and underwater sharks.

YOU'D BETTER BELIEVE IT!

The da Vinci Surgical System is a robot that assists surgeons. The robot mimics the surgeon's motions, while the surgeon sits at a console or desk near the patient. The cost of the robot is between $1 million and $2.3 million.

An engineer shakes hands with Rollin' Justin, a mobile robotics system, at a technology conference

CRYPTOLOGIST

The word "cryptology" means "the science of hiding." Cryptologists must be good mathematicians to **encrypt** information. They also need to know how to try to access encrypted information. This process might be like opening a bike lock without the combination. Cryptologists need algebra and statistics. They use **algorithms**, such as **ciphers**, that use secret codes to hide information.

Julius Caesar is the first known person to use a cipher more than 2,000 years ago. Every letter was replaced with a letter three places to the right. For example, "cat" was written "fdw." Today's ciphers used on computers turn letters into numbers and then encrypt the information.

The U.S. government has been one of the biggest employers of cryptologists. Companies also hire them to help keep customers' information secure.

YOU'D BETTER BELIEVE IT!

Navajo code talkers in World War II (1939-1945) helped the United States communicate with their allies in a secret version of their language.

encrypt—to conceal data in something by converting it to a code

algorithm—a set of instructions

cipher—an algorithm; secret writing that replaces letters with other numbers or letters to hide information

STUNT COORDINATOR

Special Skills: critical thinking, trustworthiness, good instincts, and dedication to safety

Education: not required, but most have graduated from college with a bachelor's degree in science or math

Prior Experience: no requirements, but it's helpful to have stunt work experience

Hourly Schedule: it changes daily and suddenly; can be 24/7

Salary: contract work varies widely; as a career, the average pay is $90,00 to $250,000 though some earn into the millions

The stunt coordinator's job—bottom line—is safety. A stunt coordinator uses math to prevent injury or even death.

Basic math of addition, subtraction, multiplication, and division is vital. These are used to calculate things like the distance a car travels or the height of a jump. Calculus is needed when planning stunts involving motion and force.

Using ratios is a big part of a stunt coordinator's job. For example, an actor who weighs 200 pounds (90 kilograms) might need to fly around a room on a wire. The gear needs to hold 2,000 pounds (900 kg). This is a 10 to 1 (10:1) ratio. If a rigger and an actor weigh the same, even a 2:1 ratio is the safest. This means the rigger has extra weight in case something unexpected happens.

YOU'D BETTER BELIEVE IT!

Jackie Chan is one of the few actors who coordinates his own stunts. He has injured himself on several occasions and once dislocated his cheekbone.

AERODYNAMICIST

Special Skills: understanding of forces of air and ability to solve problems

Education: at least a bachelor's degree

Prior Experience: previous work on projects

Hourly Schedule: regular full-time hours; some overtime; flexible hours if self-employed

Salary: $105,000 per year on average

An aerodynamicist studies the force of air and how it affects the motion of objects. This field is necessary when designing race cars, airplanes, and even speed skating suits. Aerodynamicists use calculations based on Sir Isaac Newton's three laws of motion. Newton wrote three books of **physics** published in 1687.

Aerodynamicists who don't do wind tunnel experiments use a lot of math. They may use trigonometry, algebra, geometry, and calculus. They work heavily with triangles. These math concepts and triangles are important when the aerodynamicist invents, tests, and improves new designs.

With racecars, for example, aerodynamicists can help improve cars' downforce. Downforce is like weight that pushes a racecar to the ground. The weight is actually airflow around the car. Cars go faster and take tighter turns with better downforce.

physics—science about motion, force, matter, and energy

Aerodynamicists need two concepts to figure out this downforce. The math concept is Bernoulli's equation. This equation is about liquid or gas flow. The other concept is the Coanda effect. This effect states that air flows around the curves of a race car. The air does not go straight. Speed is also important in these calculations.

For aircraft aerodynamicists use algebraic equations to size airplanes. First, they estimate how much weight an airplane can carry. The aircraft's body and wings are then designed, as is the size of the wing. If the weight of the airplane ends up changing, so must the design.

VISUAL EFFECTS SUPERVISOR

Almost any movie or TV show features visual effects. A fire-breathing serpent, an underwater explosion, or a spaceship engaged in battle are just a few examples. Visual effects supervisors use geometry and algebra to produce make-believe worlds that look realistic.

Most important in this field is knowledge of 3-D. Characters are made out of thousands of four-sided **polygons**. Visual effects supervisors use matrices to calculate movements. These characters and movements are placed into 3-D worlds using geometry coordinates x, y, and z. X is left to right across a screen or monitor. Y is up and down. Z points at the audience.

Knowing math also helps visual effects professionals write new computer programs using algorithms. These algorithms are the beginning of new visual effect techniques that will someday wow audiences.

polygon—in geometry a closed shape made with at least three lines

A two- or three-second movie shot can require the work of 100 or more people to bring visual effects and animation to life. Those two or three seconds can take several months to finish.

GLOSSARY

algorithm (AL-guh-rith-uhm)—a set of instructions

automaton (aw-TAH-muh-tahn)—a mechanical or moving object built centuries ago

calculus (KAL-kyuh-luhs)—a branch of mathematics that helps determine how things change

cipher (SYE-fer)—an algorithm; secret writing that replaces letters with other numbers or letters to hide information

deviation (dee-vee-EY-shuhn)—in statistics the difference between one quantity and the expected or normal quantity

encrypt (en-KRYPT)—to conceal data in something by converting it to a code

estimation (es-tuh-MAY-shuhn)—a guess made by using the information you have

forensic (fuh-REN-sik)—relating to the use of scientific knowledge or methods in solving crimes

function (FUHNGK-shuhn)—an equation with variables like x and y

integral (IN-ti-gruhl)—one of the two most basic concepts in calculus that helps determine area, volume, and lengths

matrix (MAY-triks)—in linear algebra numbers in an array, or numbers in rows and columns

physics (FIZ-iks)—science about motion, force, matter, and energy

polygon (POL-ee-gon)—in geometry a closed shape made with at least three lines

ratio (RAY-shee-oh)—a comparison of two quantities or numbers using division

slope (SLOHP)—in geometry, the steepness of a line

statistics (stuh-TISS-tiks)—information, or data, that is collected and analyzed

storyboard (STOHR-ee-bord)—a series of drawings that shows the plot of a TV show or movie

turbulence (TUR-byoo-luns)—flow or motion that is not regular or normal

READ MORE

Guillian, Charlotte. *Math*. Jobs If You Like. Chicago: Heinemann Library, 2013.

Milner Halls, Kelly. *Astronaut*. Cool Careers. North Mankato, Minn.: Cherry Lake Publishing, 2009.

INTERNET SITES

FactHound offers a safe, fun way to find Internet sites related to this book. All of the sites on FactHound have been researched by our staff.

Here's all you do:

Visit *www.facthound.com*

Type in this code: 9781491420300

CRITICAL THINKING USING THE COMMON CORE

1. Avalanche researchers work to try and help estimate the chances of future avalanches and even to prevent them from happening. What other types of natural disasters might this sort of research help us predict and even prevent? (Integration of Knowledge and Details)

2. On page 18 the text explains that Archytas created one of the first robots more than 2,000 years ago. Why do you think humans have been fascinated with robots for so long, and what do you think this means for the future? (Integration of Knowledge and Details)

INDEX